A JOURNAL FOR CHANNELING YOUR INNER ROYAL

REBECCA STOEKER

RP STUDIO

PHILADELPHIA

Copyright © 2020 by RP Studio
Illustrations copyright © 2020 by Monique Aimee
From *This Is a Book for People Who Love the Royals*, published by Running Press in 2020

Hachette Book Group supports the right to free expression and the value of copyright. The purpose of copyright is to encourage writers and artists to produce the creative works that enrich our culture.

The scanning, uploading, and distribution of this book without permission is a theft of the author's intellectual property. If you would like permission to use material from the book (other than for review purposes), please contact permissions@hbgusa.com. Thank you for your support of the author's rights.

RP Studio™
Hachette Book Group
1290 Avenue of the Americas, New York, NY 10104
www.runningpress.com
@Running_Press

Printed in China

First Edition: October 2020

Published by RP Studio, an imprint of Perseus Books, LLC, a subsidiary of Hachette Book Group, Inc. The RP Studio name and logo is a trademark of the Hachette Book Group.

The publisher is not responsible for websites (or their content) that are not owned by the publisher.

Text by Rebecca Stoeker.

Design by Jenna McBride.

ISBN: 978-0-7624-7085-3

1010

10 9 8 7 6 5 4 3 2 1

What would it be like if you could be the Queen for a day? How would your life be different? Would you change your clothes, your schedule, your food, the way you're greeted, even the way you sit? There's so much to consider when you're the one in charge—from how you'll conduct events to what you'll do to relax. In this journal you'll find an essential ten-step guide for finding *your* inner queen, plus delightful facts about the British monarchy to inspire your own royal reinvention!

Selecting the Perfect Outfit to Stand Out in a Crowd

One style rule that the Queen has held fast to over the years is adopting an outfit that is not only appropriate for the occasion, but also stands out. The Queen tends to dress in bright colors. While this is partially for safety reasons—so she is easier to spot by her security team— it also allows her to be more visible to the public. She makes a statement with every outfit she wears, standing out not only because of the bright colors but because of the confidence and dignity she exudes. Clothes send an important message about our identity and how we feel about ourselves.

Think of outfits you've worn in the past that made you feel like a show stopper. What event were you attending and what did the outfit look like? How do clothes affect your thoughts about yourself? Think about your current wardrobe. Are there some new pieces that you can invest in to spice things up? As Dr. Seuss once said, *"Why blend in when you were born to stand out?"*

The Queen starts each morning with a bath. The water must be the exact same temperature every day, measured with a thermometer, and the tub must contain exactly seven inches of water.

The Perfect Purse

❧

The Queen, except for on more glamorous occasions, almost always carries a basic, black Launer handbag. A simple black or brown handbag is a staple for any wardrobe. But packing it light is also a must. Too large or bulky of a bag can detract from a polished look. The Queen's most important items in her handbag supposedly include: a handkerchief, fountain pen, reading glasses, lipstick, a mirror, a small camera, a diary, and even a few treats for the royal corgis!

Think about your own bag. What are your royal essentials? What isn't essential that you could remove from carrying everywhere you go? It is the little details that make up the pleasing whole. Choosing to carry a smaller, less cumbersome bag might be all that is needed to take you to a more royal level of sophistication.

_____

_____

_____

_____

_____

_____

_____

_____

_____

_____

_____

_____

_____

_____

The George IV State Diadem dates back to the reign of King George IV and was designed for his coronation in 1821. The Queen wore it to her own coronation in 1953 and wears it to the State Opening of Parliament each year.

The current royal christening gown is an exact replica of the one created for Queen Victoria's firstborn, Princess Victoria, in 1841. The original gown was used by royal babies for over 150 years!

Relaxing Like a Royal

Everyone needs a break from time to time, especially the Queen! She has reigned for nearly seventy years and while to some extent she never gets a day "off," she still has places she can go for some much-needed down time. Unfortunately, one of her favorite getaways, to the Royal Yacht Britannia, no longer exists, having been decommissioned in 1997. However, her home in the Scottish Highlands, Balmoral Castle, continues to be a beloved retreat where she can relax and spend time with family. She enjoys long walks with her dogs, riding, and family picnics.

Where do you feel the most relaxed? It might not be a royal estate, but even just a room in your house or a bench at a nearby park. What activities relax you? What changes, big or small, do you think you can make in your life to increase time specifically devoted to relaxation? Remember, even the Queen sometimes needs to take a vacation!

_____

_____

_____

_____

_____

_____

_____

_____

_____

_____

_____

_____

_____

_____

_____

The Queen receives around 300 letters each day from members of the public. Ever the polite monarch, Her Majesty always tries to answer a few of them personally.

Family Focused

While not queen yet, the Duchess of Cambridge will be someday, and she already has a head start on what it means to be a queen and the demands surrounding the job. But she has also learned the importance of putting family first, even amidst the demands of royal duty. Kate comes from a very stable family that loved and supported one another. Both she and Prince William have made spending time with their children a priority and have spoken out about the importance of developing and ensuring good mental health at a young age.

What do you do daily to make family time a priority? What does your family enjoy doing together? Are there any new ideas you have for continuing to place family first? You might not be raising the future heir to the British throne, but the time you spend with your loved ones is every bit as important!

_____

_____

_____

_____

_____

_____

_____

_____

_____

_____

_____

_____

_____

_____

_____

Finding alone time can be tough when you're in charge! To find a bit of solitude, the Queen takes her beloved royal corgis for a walk around the palace grounds each day in the early afternoon.

The Queen's official residence in London, Buckingham Palace, has over 775 rooms! The queen is a remarkable monarch, who has known when to hold fast to tradition but also when to modernize—and that includes her response to the line of succession.

Timeless Traditions

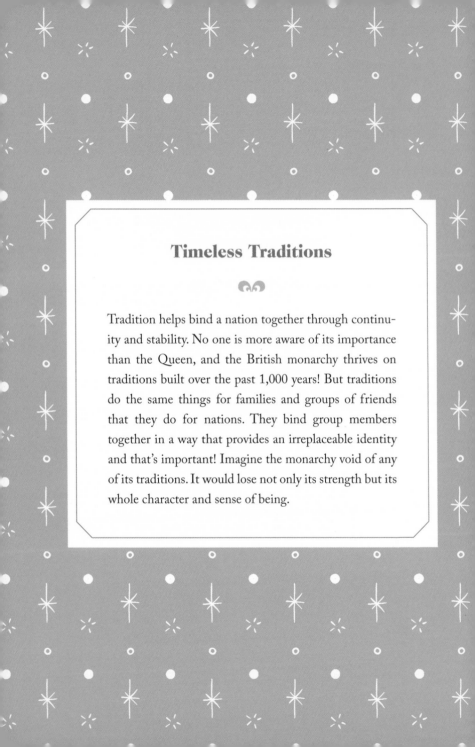

Tradition helps bind a nation together through continuity and stability. No one is more aware of its importance than the Queen, and the British monarchy thrives on traditions built over the past 1,000 years! But traditions do the same things for families and groups of friends that they do for nations. They bind group members together in a way that provides an irreplaceable identity and that's important! Imagine the monarchy void of any of its traditions. It would lose not only its strength but its whole character and sense of being.

What family traditions can you remember growing up with that you found special? What traditions does your family or close group of friends currently enjoy? Can you think of any new and unique traditions that would be fun to incorporate in the future?

_____

_____

_____

_____

_____

_____

_____

_____

_____

_____

_____

_____

_____

_____

_____

_____

In 2012, she announced the end of male-preferred primogeniture in the royal line of succession—meaning that regardless of gender, future royals will assume their place in the line based only on birth order.

Prince Philip gave then-Princess Elizabeth a diamond and platinum engagement ring, which he had designed with diamonds from a tiara that had belonged to his mother, when the pair became secretly engaged in 1946.

Stepping Away from the Spotlight

The Queen has spent her life making others feel special and important. In the hit Netflix series *The Crown* Claire Foy, who plays the Queen, says simply that the monarchy must shine, not the monarch. The Queen has staunchly adhered to this rule, understanding that one of the many roles of the monarch is to help others shine. The Queen's natural curiosity and love of people has allowed her to become an excellent conversationalist. She can effortlessly turn a conversation to focus on the other person and is an expert at avoiding sensitive and offensive subjects. Her warm smile and infectious laugh put others at ease. She is compassionate and focused on making those she meets feel valued.

What are things other people do to make you feel special? What can you do on a regular basis to make others (not just friends and family) feel important and valued? Try taking the focus off yourself and place it on someone else. There is no better feeling than making someone else feel that they truly matter.

_____

_____

_____

_____

_____

_____

_____

_____

_____

_____

_____

_____

_____

_____

_____

A coronation is a major event in the life of the monarch! The monarch sits in King Edward's Chair, which has been used in every coronation since 1626—though the chair itself was made in the year 1300—and is anointed by the Archbishop of Canterbury.

The tradition of brides wearing white for their wedding days began with a famously trendsetting royal—Queen Victoria! She chose white for her wedding in 1840 to show off the exquisite lace on her gown—made by struggling British lace makers whose work she wished to highlight.

Devotion to Diligence

One of the most defining traits of the Queen's reign has been her diligence and unwavering devotion to duty. For example, every day for her whole reign (except for Christmas and Easter) she spends a few hours going through one of the red leather governmental boxes. These contain state papers, memos, and summaries of Parliamentary debates, among other things. Once while visiting a friend, she had to excuse herself to take time to go through her daily box. The friend asked if she truly had to and the Queen replied, "If I missed one once, I would never get it straight again." Rain or shine, at sea or on land, a red box is delivered.

What are you good at sticking to and being diligent with in life? What are some areas that you'd like to improve on and how might you go about doing so? Having a game plan that is practical, reasonable, and doable goes a long way in helping us meet our goals!

_____

_____

_____

_____

_____

_____

_____

_____

_____

_____

_____

_____

_____

_____

_____

Queen Elizabeth II has hundreds of royal events each year—but even on a windy day, the Queen does not have to worry about an unfortunate wardrobe malfunction at these engagements, as she has tiny weights sewn into the hems of her dresses!

An Established Royal Routine

While the Queen is often seen at numerous and varied events throughout the week, her life behind palace doors runs very much according to established routines that have remained the same for decades. Routines give the Queen (and us) a sense of balance and normalcy amongst life's ever-changing and often chaotic tide. Routines help our minds remain steady and focused. Here is a quick look at the Queen's daily schedule:

The Queen rises promptly at 7:30 am every day, enjoying a cup of Earl Gray tea before a bath at 8:00 am. Breakfast is served at 8:30 am and the Queen then attends to various royal duties before taking the royal pups for a walk at 12:30 pm. Lunch is served promptly at 1:00 pm, with public royal engagements usually taking place in the afternoon. High tea is served at 5:00 pm and, on Wednesdays, the Queen meets with the prime minister at 6:30 pm. She writes in her diary every night and usually goes to bed around 11:00 pm.

What established routines do you currently follow on a daily basis? Are there areas where you think you could improve your quality of life through adding more routine and stability? What steps can you take to make more established routines in life a reality? No one expects you to have the same regimental lifestyle that the Queen requires, but some established routines are necessary and very beneficial!

_____

_____

_____

_____

_____

_____

_____

_____

_____

_____

_____

_____

_____

_____

Traditionally, members of the royal family have always given birth at home. All of the Queen's four children were born at home—though at which royal residence has always varied since there are so many residences to choose from!

When you're the Queen, you set the menu! At the palace there are certain items that will never be on offer, such as shellfish and garlic (the Queen is known to dislike garlic and never allows it served in her meals).

Keep Calm and Carry On

Both the Queen and the Duchess of Cambridge have seemingly learned to develop a "keep calm and carry on" attitude about life. Rather than being governed by emotions, they are governed by correct actions. Emotions can change daily, hourly, or even by the minute! While emotions are important and shouldn't be entirely ignored, their notorious changeability makes them poor leaders. They make much better followers, and right emotions almost always follow right actions.

The Queen knows that an emotional monarchy would be disastrous and would never provide the strength and continuity that the people desperately need in a monarch. The monarch is an emblem of unwavering stability in the midst of ever-changing times. The Queen has learned that showing some emotion makes her endearing and relatable, but too much emotion can cause instability and errors in judgment. The people want a monarch to show the steadiness and strength that we often long for ourselves during hard times. The positive legacy of the Queen's reign lies in her ability to make informed judgements to best serve her people. While the old adage, "follow your heart" sounds beautiful, it is the Queen's ability to follow her head, with a kind heart in quick step behind it, that allows her to reign successfully.

Life is all about finding the proper balance. What areas in your life are causing unnecessary stress and preventing you from being able to "keep calm and carry on"? What techniques or actions can you use to help keep you calm and keep your emotions in check in the midst of life's never-ending stress? Music? A warm bath? A jog? Make whatever those actions/techniques are a priority in helping to clear your mind and allow it to carry on making wise decisions outside the realm of often misleading emotions.

_____

_____

_____

_____

_____

_____

_____

_____

_____

_____

_____

_____

_____

_____

The Queen has an impressive array of tiaras! One of the most famous, the Cartier Halo Scroll Tiara, was originally given to the Queen Mother by her husband, King George VI, and then passed on to the Queen (then Princess Elizabeth) on her eighteenth birthday. It is most well-known today as the tiara that the Catherine Middleton wore on her wedding day to Prince William in 2011.

Service Made Simple

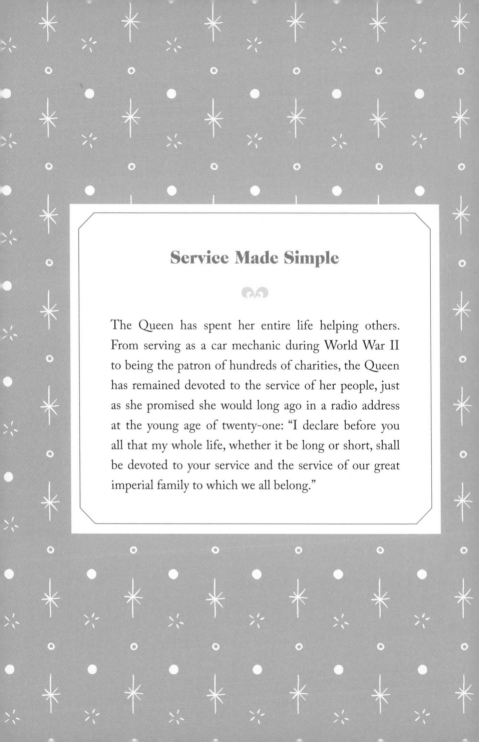

The Queen has spent her entire life helping others. From serving as a car mechanic during World War II to being the patron of hundreds of charities, the Queen has remained devoted to the service of her people, just as she promised she would long ago in a radio address at the young age of twenty-one: "I declare before you all that my whole life, whether it be long or short, shall be devoted to your service and the service of our great imperial family to which we all belong."

How do you serve those close to you and those in your community? How do you give of your time and energies to improve the lives of those around you? Remember, you don't have to be an actual queen to make a difference. You just have to *want* to make a difference!

_____

_____

_____

_____

_____

_____

_____

_____

_____

_____

_____

_____

_____

_____

_____

_____

Kensington Palace, a sprawling residence in London, is not home to the monarch but is often referred to as the "royal dormitory" due to the many other members of the family who reside there.

Endnotes

1   Clark, Lucie. "5 Fascinating Facts About The Queen's Handbag Habits." *Vogue*, 19 Aug. 2019, www.vogue.com.au/fashion/accessories/4-fascinating-facts-about-the-queens-handbag-habits/image-gallery/d0b7e59aebfbce9da246dd49bbf23e92.

2   "A Sombre Farewell." *The Royal Yacht Britannia*, The Royal Yacht Britannia, 2019, www.royalyachtbritannia.co.uk/about/royal-residence/decommission/.

3   Taylor, Elise. "All You Need to Know About Balmoral, the Queen's Scottish Summer Castle." *Vogue*, 22 Aug. 2019, www.vogue.com/article/balmoral-scotland-queen-elizabeth-castle-royals.

4   Bedell Smith, Sally. *Elizabeth The Queen: The Life of a Modern Monarch*. Random House, 2012, pp. 71-72.

5   "Inside Queen Elizabeth II's Jam-Packed Daily Schedule." *US Weekly*, 3 Jan. 2019, www.usmagazine.com/celebritynews/news/inside-queen-elizabeth-iis-jam-packed-daily-schedule/.

6   "A Speech by the Queen on her 21st Birthday, 1947." *The Official Website of the British Royal Family*, The Royal Household of Buckingham Palace, 2019, www.royal.uk/21st-birthday-speech-21-april-1947.